MW00934411

Heartbeat

POEMS FOR MEDITATION

~

William J. Rewak, S.J.

ISBN: 1978483732
ISBN-13: 9781978483736
Library of Congress Control Number: 2017916641
CreateSpace Independent Publishing Platform
North Charleston, South Carolina

Ad Majorem Dei Gloriam

Table of Contents

Preface · xi
Prologue · xiii
Heartbeat · xv

Part I: God's Design · 1

You Alone · 3
Package · 4
My Webster · 6
Evening Walk · 8
Lighter Moments · 10
Autumn · 11
Hummingbird · 12
The Stain · 13
Playing Scrabble · 14
White Swans · 15
Transfiguration · 17
Solitaire · 19
The Terrible Point · 21
Daisies · 23
Marathon · 24
Chapel At Midnight · 25
Psalm 139 · 26

The Egret · 27
Certitude · 28
A Word · 29
Happiness · 30
Whisper At Noon · 32
On Knees · 34
Design · 35
A Black And White Terrier · 36
Here At The Altar · 38

Part II: His Life · 39

The First Day · 41
Like Any Ten-Year-Old · 43
Higher Things · 45
Joseph · 46
You Took Time · 47
Mountain Words · 49
Fine Wine · 51
The Barnyard · 52
Golgotha · 54
On The Morning · 56
Eucharist At Emmaus · 58
They Say You Are Risen · 59

Part III: Friends · 61

Bartimaeus · 63
Homespun · 64
Ignatius At La Storta · 65
For Margaret Clitherow And Her Unborn, Martyred
In York On March 25, 1586 · 67
Remembering El Salvador Jesuit Martyrs Of November 16, 1989 · · · · 69

Like Julian · 71
Missa Solemnis · 72

Epilogue · 75
"Our Hearts Are Restless Till They Rest In Thee" · · · · · · · · · · · · · · 77

Notes For Part III · 80

Acknowledgments · 83

Preface

DENISE LEVERTOV, IN HER BOOK of poems, *The Stream and the Sapphire*, wrote that she did not ordinarily issue thematic collections; she chose to fill her books with poems that touch upon a variety of themes. Presumably, she did so to provide the reader with as many doors to open as possible. And such is the case with most poets. But for *The Stream and the Sapphire*, she gathered together many of the religiously-themed of her poems in order to afford easy access for those of her readers who were interested in issues of faith and spirituality.

This present book is an attempt to do the same. Many of the poems here have appeared in my previous books, but many of them are new. They touch upon the difficulties, and the joy, of prayer; the sacredness of the mundane; how all language ultimately inches toward the one Word. There are poems that honor special saints, and there is a section on various events in the life of Christ – and there is even a parable. There are poems that both question and honor the mystery of God.

They are poems for meditation.

Bill Rewak, S.J.

Prologue

Heartbeat

I want to tell You:

I enjoy this walk along the shore
You reach into my words and cleanse them
You know my sentences and build them
into the praise I owe You

You startle my tongue so I speak as You wish
You guide me in the minutes I scatter
around my day and You show the steps
I take, the stairs I climb, You show me the faces
I hold in hope, the eyes I know are Yours

You are the life I seek in the corners and alleys
of my striving and though I walk with a strained
    heart
I know Your hand is only a heartbeat away.

PART I:

God's Design

You Alone

Help me now, Lord,
to say this prayer
so it is not forced
through the eye
of a needle but
has a wide avenue
arched with magnolias:
that You alone
hold this flesh
in Your hand so
it does not flake
that You alone
know the desire
that so often
veers aside
but rights itself
time and again
because You alone
can fill every want
and there is no wall
anymore, just
a small space
I have to cross
so small I can reach
with a whisper of love.

Package

We wonder
what You think of us;

not talking about love,
talking about thinking:

when You have time
(there's a conundrum)

do You ponder the black stars
in our minds,

do You examine the steps
we never take,

do You sit up and take notice
when we graft a rose?

When we're driving a freeway,
do You check our pulse;

do You agree with the morning's hairdo
and the flannel shirt?

Does all that, indeed,
take time?

Where do You take time?
Do You travel with it

here on our time-encrusted
lump of clay?

Here's my own take:
You don't need time.

We shouldn't worry.
It's all one package.

My Webster

This dictionary is so hard to lift:
it's filled with the literature of the ages,

the correspondence of millennia, the recipes
of all gustatorial delights, and the bland

instructions for every gadget we've surrounded
ourselves with. It is a compendium of history

and a theological insight into the business
of God. There it sits on my bookshelf,

intimidating, quiet, deeply proud
of itself. But I tell you, my smug Webster,

that this morning's prayer could not find
the words it struggled for and though I paged

carefully and even tried a magnifying glass
I could give neither the pain of absence

nor the joy of presence a proper language.
Can it be my magnifying glass is not strong

enough, or are there words hidden behind
words? Have we yet to discover a vocabulary

trying to inch its way out of the chrysalis
of desire?

Evening Walk

It's difficult
as leaves blow
late in the day
and the path
loses itself
in quiet rustling
and the soft footfalls
       of other beasts
to know if
You're walking here too
or if the light touch
is just
       the dark air
that wraps
around itself;
such words
as these
are meant to clarify
but who would
resort to lines
       of letters
              carefully stitched
who would depend
on such
       fabrication
to learn Your mystery;
       walking

is a better contrivance
as leaves lift
and float
and turn their colors
before they fall.

Lighter Moments

I'm sitting here with a piece of chocolate
and marshmallow squeezed together like a pie
and thinking, this is the best it can be -
but then I think how superficial my life's goals
must be if I can be content with a pop
of chocolate; but then I think that's superficial,
too, because it's often the lighter moments
of life that light up the daily stint,
that show us there are sparks inside the meanest
and I can revel in "Peanuts" and "Blondie" for they
    touch
a string that ought to be played more often,
and perhaps if it were we'd see them as grace.

Autumn

I stopped on my walk today
and looked at the small yellow

gingko leaves scattered across
the sidewalk; their tree had let them fall:

too heavy for an aging fellow
who had lost his taste for adornment.

They were left to fend for themselves
and would soon be swept away

by an orderly caretaker, hired to deal
with leavings. I brought one to my room

and caressed it, its silkiness soft
on my skin; I hold it now and watch

the fan-like edge abandon its life.

Hummingbird

A hummingbird
in the heart
You are,
magical and light,
settling softly,
but quick to note
the ripples,
to tend them;
in a movement
so swift
You can fly
and leave us
waiting
on the edge
of forgetfulness,
wandering,
until Your wings,
invisible,
alight again.

The Stain

Is there a stain on the soul?

A mark handed to us as a butcher
would serve a loin of beef,
with no cost, freely given?

Do our souls limp
at their first breath?

Or do we begin as elemental
Billy Budds, open
to the whims of a wind
whipping the sails of our lives
into darker waters?

Billy kept it free to the end
but there are some here
in our travels who revel in the wind
and they always have the upper hand,

it seems.

Where is the soul
with no stain? Does it always
swing, under the sun,
from a grieving yardarm?

Playing Scrabble

"To gain your life, you must lose it"
Matthew 16:25

Did you ever play Scrabble with
God?
It's unnerving because
words started with
God
in a scarlet blast one morning
and things like sun and peaches
formed into meaning
but there were bigger things like
algebra, gravity, and desire
that needed articulation and
God
had a job classifying it all
so we could sit and ponder
this delightful play
but the inventor has the upper hand
so even making happy moves
I always lose with
God.

White Swans

Pause now
and watch:

the sun's ready
to shine, to drop

sparkles, ignite
each house

with early dawn
with the song

of larks rising,
wait and see

if such a song
can steal

into my heart
melt the old

shackles and reveal
a desire, clear

and just, pure
as the white swans

of Stratford, agile
as a wing aloft,

so I'm ready to greet
the day You've set

aside for me.

Transfiguration

See the daffodils out there:
their long-stemmed insistence
on being first

and the small green knobs
pushing against the earth

we know it happens
often, rain clouds
step aside
and bow to a day of light -
but surprise, always,
ice shifts into sun:

farther down than we can go
lies the straining bulb

not a thing to re-plant
but a Word to explode
break into colors
that leap through centuries
of gravel, of wrong turns
to be our yellow umbrellas

this breath that hallows

this gift that splits the old
worn rocks
and flowers in our prayer.

Solitaire

I racked up a big number on Solitaire
this afternoon, jumping back and forth

between tens and jacks and hoping for a clean
sweep from ace to king or vice

versa, then noticed José in the yard
sweeping everything into a dip in the lawn

and I like the idea of cleansing, it's the application
of morality to the detritus of everyday life;

like the sweeping changes periodically called for
in the halls of government; though the metaphor of game,

I was warned, does not fit exactly,
that God does not tinker that way,

but I imagine tinker toys are as much
a part of God's creation as fiery nebulae

so sin, Solitaire, and sweeping are not discrete,
they find their meaning in those desert sands

we dream of, drifting in with a voice
that urged we enter a new dimension

by bowing before a burning bush; silly
perhaps to engage that story? but in a tale

that risks derision is found a flame
that purifies every game.

The Terrible Point

You never know
where you're going
when you pray:
buses honk
and pages turn,
people run in front
and trip intentions;
it takes time
to pause, reach
into silence, but
once there,
a train takes over
and the terrible point
is you can't direct
the driver, a wizard
who sits dark
behind a hard partition -
not like the movie,
with green smoke
(but with truer magic).
Along the way,
you stop, get out
and walk around the dancers,
watch the fireflies;
a trumpet sounds,
insistent, so you jump
and try the journey again.

No other traveler
for company, just a box
filled with notes and books,
carved animals and canes,
and still they take up
space you want
for other things,
for wondering how
you got aboard,
or how the train winds
its way without a map.

Daisies

Why didn't I stop at daisies?
A blushing yellow core with a myriad

of "He loves me, He loves me nots"
spreading out in honor; there,

you see, I wanted to ensure you were not
left in suspense, hanging over the valley

of My indecision; that would have been unkind
like the old milkman dropping off a spot

of skim milk (as marvelous a part
of the cow as that is) instead of adding cream

and cottage cheese, too; so I added
the iris - figure that one out! -

the mystic rose and the snooty orchid
and, watch for it, the obedient bluebell

because I wanted the question decided.
And I have more up my sleeve.

Marathon

For example:

the toothpaste we use each morning
or the telephone on the neat desk when ringing
the DVD of Hercule Poirot playing murderously
the sharing of a plate of bread

hoof beats on tile

the scribbles we make to schedule our day

all actions that by their unimportance prove
the importance of Your presence;

the energies of life
are laddered meditations
we climb to find You.
We cannot be misguided: feeble
steps beget a marathon.

Chapel At Midnight

Do You wait for us to visit?
Is there longing or rest?

Is there a silence inside of silence
You indulge in while alone?

Here in the dark of candles
no breath of breathing

just the air of a loneliness
filled with the tumult You know;

does this emptiness give You
space You need to prepare for us?

Psalm 139

When I sit and when I stand?
Every muscle movement watched,
cared for? This is the nut:

that even a reaching of a hand,
the slicing of an apple to let the juice
flow, this moment of silence -

all matter for the quilt
You sew. My stretching (a new stitch),
my speaking (a new red) -

a fancy You formed that flies
heedless of better intent
and creates a world You forgive -

these gather to lie side
by side in wondrous witness
to the touch of Your grace.

The Egret

An egret stepped warily into the trattoria
on the corner and ordered a pasta with marinara;
the clientele paused as one pauses
when cocktail chatter is broken by a belch
or as happened the previous evening when a rhinoceros
waddled in for a martini: it was getting increasingly
difficult to eat without the odd interruption.
The owner (a Neapolitan) was open-minded:
he believed meals have a spiritual flavor
relished by all of God's kingdom,
that a table is the communal center of creation.
But his diners refused to countenance feathers
and snorts, to extend their fellowship to those
considered less favored in the chain of being.
Rumors spread about his tasteless predilection.
He lost business. The egret, though,
a snowy delight in his dark day,
chattered on about marketing, new customers,
seasoned opportunities, a unique vision
in an expanding world of gustation.
The Neapolitan - who first saw light
at the edge of a vast uncornered sea -
stood in the night and watched
the still stars, so far away.
They stayed bright, no matter
the turning of the world. He nodded,
returned to his kitchen, brushed the cobwebs,
and told the egret to open all the doors.

Certitude

They offered it to me free: I walked in through the blue door and was greeted by a red-lipped teen-ager who took my name and asked me why I was born. I must have mistaken her words, so mellifluous they seemed, but she asked again and I said it was God's decision but what I really want is a new iPhone; she took me by the arm and in the shadows of a corner protected by samples of iPhones, earphones, iPads and other wonders that have re-drawn the contours of our lives she asked if I was serious about God; well, I said, of course, and she said she had once rolled in waves off a beach in Maui and was caught in a maelstrom of bubbles and her life had since never been bubble-free, so she thought maybe God was a harsh creator of bubbles and did not care how they interrupted a daily swim; well, I was flabbergasted and hesitantly said perhaps bubbles are not the troubles you think they are but little pearls to breeze your skin lightly and show you the colors that burst through the mist each morning, and she looked at me and brushed a speck of dirt off her sleeve, then sighed and said that if we knew how the bubbles were born we could discern their purpose, and that is the point, she said; well, I was nonplussed, so I hitched up my pants and was about to give her a dose of homiletic certitude when she asked, "How may I help you today?"

A Word

Can we dare trees to speak,
the ocean to bellow a reason?

Can we ask the farthest star
to unveil its light and show us
what lies behind its orbit?

Are we asking too much
that creation open its secrets?

Each day, wandering
an evening coastline, orange
and yellow in dying hours,

we wait for a language we can decipher,
that its words can speak

to our words and we'll know
why the heart beats faster
in the soft light, when sun and

moon are there together,
when all language is but the Word.

Happiness

Roaming through my years I'm trying to figure out
when it was I first full-throat-out laughed

because I couldn't contain my happiness and I find
an evening, its darkness weirdly crinkled

with throbbing red lights from the roller coaster
a mile away, when I lay in bed with David Copperfield's

courage and a dish of a sliced-up Milky Way
on the blanket beside me, and I'm thinking, "Was this it?"

The still simplicity of the event, like a yellow leaf
lying spent from an autumn wind, makes me shudder,

as if I cannot take life seriously enough or as if
life itself holds no mysteries for me, but I know

I lay there with my heart full of Dickens' love
for this child and my tongue wrapped around a Milky Way

as if it slaked a hunger for my own words,
and all of it - coupled with a loneliness I reveled in

and the warmth of the bed on this cool evening –
made me smile and then laugh: I knew

at that small minute how happiness could steal in
and forge a soul that had been waiting.

Whisper At Noon

If you look deep down
into the heart of a diamond,
you'll see a speck of unrest:

it's struggling to shine;
for all of its glory, it itches
to achieve the one dazzling

stone in all the universe
that can never be repeated,
the one flower that will send

its aroma to the farthest galaxy
and be honored for the task.
There are other things

we need to know if we are
to survive: why redwoods
can be cut but never tamed,

how oceans feed us, why God
steps around us gingerly
and sculpts our facets with precision

why evening light recalls
a death. We plunge into reality
at birth and begin:

there are lilacs along the road
fireflies at night
a whisper at noon.

On Knees

For Alan Kurdi, a 3-year-old Syrian boy
who drowned in the Mediterranean on
September 2, 2015, while seeking a home

Groaning from the corners, hurrying of steps
along the wall, black sighs in the hawthorn

bushes; this is the language we hear on the hour,
the insistent and apocalyptic murmurs that harass

our days; we ask, humbly, is the Cross
the only and permanent avenue we travel?

We are on knees, we have not turned our faces
from You, we have lifted our morning eyes

in love, but worms are moving, snakes
climb trees, sparks blow in

from across the water; where is the saint's speech?
Where the trustful gleam from a child's eye?

The tsunami overwhelms so there is no speech or sight;
are we not ashamed to watch as You weep?

Design

I was walking
down the stairs
last night

when I thought of You

those moments come
swifter now:
when I lather my chin
in the morning
when I look into Your face
in class
when the evening closes
on a Lifesaver

these things I know
they're fabric of the day

and I press for the design to show.

A Black And White Terrier

I was on my way
to Mass yesterday
when a black and white

terrier stepped out
from behind a wall
and looked at me

as if he wanted to know
my name and as if
he was about to give

me his; I thought it
odd he should be concerned,
as if he knew I was playing

through my purpose
and getting up nerve
to make a decisive

move, so I sat
on the curb and riffled
his ears and told him

what he wanted
to know, hoping
that such a revelation

would nudge me
closer to a decision,
but though I did not see

in his large brown
eyes any answer,
I spied a gleam of hope.

Here At The Altar

Here at the altar I stand and I wonder: why
do my fingers not burn when I hold You, why
does the wood not burst, the windows not splinter
into mirrors reflecting a thousand tongues of flame;
why are the gardens still and the day silent;
how do we walk straight afterwards?

Lesser events have toppled nations;
I would have expected You to earthquake
my own world, but it continues gently and with patience;
is a fissure, rent in time, able to hide itself so well,
in an ordinary day, that we cannot perceive
moments of fire in this breaking of bread?

PART II:
His Life

The First Day

In that moment
when You stepped onto our earth
was sound something new:
the bleating of sheep,
the soft swish of wind, a voice
that blanketed You with whispers
of joy;
did You see, for the first time, the sparkles
and colors of the night?

Did her face fill Your eyes?
When You felt the strength
that kept Your body warm,
did you turn in wonder?

Were You pleased
with the freshness of a word,
how shadows moved,
the sure ground they all stood on
(the dense texture of wood)?

Did You smell the straw
and could You taste the evening?

Did You see a toy in a winging dove?

Was it all a great surprise?

You stretched Your hand to touch
and You found it good.

Like Any Ten-Year-Old

He skipped along the lane
like any ten-year-old,
brushing the tares as he went,
whistling a tune he'd heard

last Sabbath, marveling
at how it climbed to a wonder
he could not reach, then catching up
with two others to wander down

by the riverbank to watch fishermen
clean their night's work,
learning, always, as boys do,
the antics and duties of men.

He cupped the warm sand
in his hand, feeling its grit
and trying to count each
grain but guessing they were as numerous

as the midnight stars of the heavens.
The three of them offered to hold
the nets for washing, and hc noted,
with frank curiosity, how the sweat

of the fishermen fell on the nets,
how it glistened in the morning sun,

and the joy he felt as their laughter
shortened and blessed their work.

Each day, a new scene
to tuck away for the future.
And all this, if they could but see,
was the glory of the Lord.

Higher Things

Jesus had a scar
on his arm
where a saw flipped
and tried to bite
through muscle
and I want to know
if this scar
was pre-ordained
I want to know
if the saw was fixed
or if even on
Jesus
accidents fell
to urge our minds
to higher things.

Joseph

You didn't mind
when he went about
his Father's business

a puzzle, of course,
for he was your son, too,
and you loved him

you showed him
edges on the wood
and how it would curl

you fashioned the joinings
so two dimensions
made three, you gave him

the tools to build
but the home he built
stands on Golgotha

you could not know
how he would use
your gift.

You Took Time

You took time to walk away
and climb the hill
settle down and review
the day

to check Your words

recall the young man
who could not see

the gentle Pharisee
deep in his faith
who could not see

Peter who needed
Your words to settle
his bluster and mold
his heart

you bowed to Your Father
and asked for strength

because this little world
was the unlikely
scene of grace

it was the mirror of His love
and lifted every wound
for healing, every nail
for a blessing

here on this hill
You built your resolve
and carried it down
to the valley

so they could share Your life.

Mountain Words

It had been a busy day, people hobbling
       crowds with bad breath
children though were a light
when they ran the world opened
       exploded
and laughter fell into everyone
he loved all, no doubt,
he ached to heal, to enfold
in the strength of a Samson
       but so needed
              a gap in time
                    to listen
here on this mountain where he learned
the echoes in the slight breeze
white rustlings
       of the night
he could feel life, as always,
be with his Father who knew
the strain, the pulling out of himself:
would there be, he asked, an end
he could relish
       would muscle hold?
and each morning his eyes
brought flame
each morning his hands would lift

in age-old prayers
each morning his words flexed
        hard
as the stones of Golgotha.

Fine Wine

He felt sometimes he was talking to wood
   to scarecrows
   hay-for-brains
he loved them but they could not imagine
   his plight.
He spent dusty hours on roads of Galilee
words spilled out hour by hour
and they lapped it up thinking it milk
   when it was fine wine.
At night when moonlight was hesitant
and the waves of Genesaret fell asleep
he'd walk the sand and hold the scent
of evening blossoms
   in his hand
and feel his Father close:
   that healed the wounds.
At daybreak he'd try again
he'd try again with a grain of wheat.

The Barnyard

So bring them all in, gather the geese,
chickens, the donkey, make room for the cow

even the annoying rooster who hasn't
a good word for anyone, empty the barnyard,

we want all of you to be safe here where
the fire burns warm and we can enjoy

your company; it's not often a guest arrives
so sit quietly while we bathe his feet and mix

the corn; I've heard his glance can turn a head
and make granite blanch; I've heard his touch

can paralyze the underworld, his word can halt
lightning; but do not be intimidated, he wants

only a rest and welcomes your comments
because you, too, have a stake in this endeavor;

you, too, note human folly but have always
remained still: now, speak up and air your

wisdom, let him know he has friends who will
guard his walk, carry him along the lane,

crow when a traitorous word is spoken.
He is happy to receive any help you can give.

Golgotha

Did you know me
when you held me?

You would remember
the night blinking
the lamb that would not leave
the riotous travelers
elbowing their way
the seraphic music
of a rustling breeze
and morning larks
fluttering to see;

the joyous caress
of a new hand;

but did you know
in this dark place
when I came from you
that the straw and dust
would remain
that the bewildered
silence of strangers
would remain?

Could you read the signs
in my eyes?

Did you know
the steps I would take
away from you
but hold you all those days
all the nights I prayed?

Did you know
I would calm the seas
and give life to a friend?

Did you know
I have lived your life inside
and every leaf I touch
is a grace because of you?

Did you know
you prepared my walk
up this last hill?

Did you know me
when you held me?

On The Morning

She had often thought about Isaiah's banquet
of the Lord and wondered if there was a place
set for her; here, she ate her morning bread,

swept out the dust that filled
the corners of her room, then sitting in silence
she'd look into the clouds for the soft rain

that would fall on the hills and bring comfort;
she waited for a word that would lift the day
and envied the sparrows that knew their flight,

the long sweet grass that accepted
each season of birth and death,
the skipping lambs that never questioned;

an uneasiness gripped her in the tight evenings
as she heard dark whispers in the halls
of her heart and watched the shadows follow

the fluttering dance of her candle flame;
she woke often only to hear the click
of insects and the untroubled murmur of doves.

Then one day, beside the lake,
a word came to her and she turned to catch
all its inflections, gathering them in with hope,

storing them in a safe place where she could fondle
them at ease. Their memory accompanied her
and made her so bold that when he looked at her

she said, "Yes." The days after, she followed
and walked and listened; she served meals
and used her own words to guide

those in search of a shepherd, she led to him
the poor who opened their emptiness, she taught
a new prayer that asked for forgiveness.

Walking beside him often, she watched
how he touched a brow and made the whole
come to life, how a glance would change

a life. But it didn't last: she found herself
on a hill, catching his blood in her hands
and wondering if all she had invested was a dream.

On the morning, she sat in the garden and looked
ahead to the sweeping, the insects and doves
and knew that rain could bring no comfort.

A voice startled her, she turned but could not see;
then: "Mary." And everything lifted,
her place was set at last.

Eucharist At Emmaus

They should have known because they had
the news - though admittedly the women were excited

and hard to parse - but they walked away
and trudge now down dusty lanes

feeling sorry for themselves. Was there some regret
at all the time spent so far?   No, more

of a heartbreak for one they had loved. A tornado
had touched down and lifted the roofs off

all they had built, splintered the furniture
they had faithfully assembled, left them

wandering. But – later, they will recall a softer
breeze from behind, a fragrance of life,

and words that cheered like a happy tale will cheer
little children and fill their imagination

with something new, tell their spirits
there are reasons, so they can sit at a meal

and discover another dimension – and more:
receive flesh and blood.

They Say You Are Risen

"I shall not die but live" (Psalm 118)

They say You are risen
and walk these streets;
I know the blood here -
it runs acid on flesh
I see tar melting in the sun
as bare feet struggle
I know the shadows
of lifted arms
all hangs on my soul
the loss of what should have been.

They say You are risen
and sit in our homes;
I know the floors grimed
cold
the rooms whose doors
are cobwebs
I know the grass, afraid
to approach
the small cries
lifting in an embarrassed night.

They say You are risen
and touch the foreheads
of those in battle

we know the dimensions
of each bullet
feel the hot sand
we know the fallen names
and dead ends
annals cannot erase
the words of those who are left.

They say You are risen:
if You are, do you weep?
Once, You sat on a hill
above Jerusalem, tears
fell for those who could not see
will there be a time,
shortly, when Your smile
will be the games we play
Your joy our labor
will there be a time?

PART III:

Friends

Bartimaeus

Mark 10:46

"I want to see," he said
then looking around he saw faces
         staring
and one face welcoming;
he could not describe the face -
"dark, a beard certainly," but
he saw now with new eyes
the eyes of one who opens eyes:
they held the darkness of the farthest
         planet
they held the spark of a new
         Isaiah.
To see was everything, every morning's
         promise
now he could stand straight
and walk true
so he picked up his discarded cloak
and walked with Him.

In each village, for years, he explained
the contours of the face
         he remembered
and had come to know.

Homespun

Poor Clare!
They wanted you to wear
>   silk
and all you wanted was to share
>   a dream.
They thought it fuzzy
even frumpy
>   wrinkled;
but you washed and then pressed
with hot stones its smooth strength.
Your homespun dream wrote history.

Ignatius At La Storta

There, in the halls of Loyola,
he couldn't find the word

stuck somewhere
in the middle of his tongue

he could feel it trying to speak:
though he wrestled with flames

inside, caught by their beauty
scarred by their power,

he walked mute.
Soon, he found sentences

in Manresa and Paris
in polyglot Venice;

he traded them with friends
jiggled them to find their core.

Then one morning
he sat, sandals worn,

and words fell from the silent
walls of La Storta

they tumbled, hurrying
and the moment limned his life:

bid now to share peace in castles
malls and bus depots, he could

limp like a new Jacob,
holding stronger shoulders,

with a new step, a new Word.

For Margaret Clitherow And Her Unborn, Martyred In York On March 25, 1586

Down a lane lined with silver birches
she walks, this Margaret I admire, this
Margaret, unafraid of the Queen's reach,

intent only on the Word to be sown
among the bluebells and snowdrops she loves,
carrying inside her the new life

that each morning warms her smile –
O Margaret, they have already prepared
the blanket that will leave you cold:

a door, rocks pulled out from under
the dogwood and Scots pine, harshness
culled from the quiet beauty of your land.

Knowledge was always there, ticking,
itching, reminding you of the broken end
you had long divined was yours.

I stand in your room, centuries after,
and marvel that from such simplicity
arose such determined grace,

that from the butcher's broom huddling
around your life you learned strength
to equal the weight that bore down

on you and your unborn, that from the grit
of York, such a pearl could shine. I marvel
that my own prayers are lit from your flame.

Remembering El Salvador Jesuit Martyrs Of November 16, 1989

"These martyrs were killed for the way they lived,
that is, for how they expressed their faith in love."
Dean Brackley, S.J.

I am a garden
Yo soy un jardín
I grow the *Flor de Izote* and *Loroco*
and orchids that blush with morning's light
seeds are deep in me
        they die
and then burst into the colors I love

I am one with every world of spring

I glow in the sunlight
and dance in the breeze
I lie open to what my gardener desires

but seeds are different
and there are different desires:
that grieving day
eight seeds fell on my soil

there were footsteps and clamoring
the breeze had stilled

so harsh sounds ricocheted
and my dust hung lifeless in the air
my autumn leaves shriveled

I felt the weight of impress
of possible new planting.

Now, I grow stronger
and bloom with a fresh grace
        each year
petals livelier than before
send their scent
out on an eager breeze

to tell the news:

Yo soy un jardín nuevo.

Like Julian

We are blessed when the rain falls,
blessed when the waves of the ocean
rise above us and salute the stars,
when the hand of a child holds us
and we are warmed; we are blessed
with the lilies of summer, the vine-filled
hills of autumn: how could we not
leap in gratitude?

                    Julian of Norwich
in her cold cell reveled in the warmth
of the Child and in her sure prayer
she reached to her heaven and begged
for light: it surrounded her and she breathed
in its fragrance, bowing to the One
she sought through the winters of her land.

How do we, in this soft climate, deserve
that light? How do the blessings that fall
each day that form a groove in our lives,
that scar our skin, mark us for You
so we cannot walk away, so that like Julian
we are captured, enrolled among the saints?

Missa Solemnis

"Introibo ad altare Dei"

These steps are worn, sanded by the sandals
of the years, the pages I read are crisp and grey,

but the words inch into life as they did
when Ambrose lifted the cup;

even the scarred wooden altar in Sangchuan
still shines with glory.

The deepest plunge of our yearning,
the taproot of how we live, finds its rock here,

in the warm gestures of the everyday ritual
we sometimes glide through as a dutiful memory

or attend to because of current need,
but life erupts when least we look

and the wild solemnity of song or word
captures the heart, imprisons it so we cannot

through sin or distraction or boredom
escape.

Then Ambrose and Xavier stand with us,
holding the Eternal,

revealing what knits together
the sometimes frayed strands

of a tender faith.

Epilogue

"Our Hearts Are Restless Till They Rest In Thee"

(St. Augustine)

Bees buzzing
and whales breaching,
hummingbirds flitting
from daisies to tulips,

shoppers rushing
with open purses
from Macy's to Louis
Vuitton, comets

streaking and stars
exploding, a horde
of our creatures wandering
in a restless fever

trying to reap
the juice Augustine
spoke of, trying
to capture the stillness

at the heart, deep
in the volcanos, encased
in the hurricanes, in tectonic
plates searching

for their fit, my own
blood impatient,
rushing in circles -
all pulsing

and urging toward a moment
of rest, a moment
when the tearing will heal,
the fabric hold.

Notes For Part III

Page 64: "Poor Clare": In the year 1212, St. Clare of Assisi, with the help of St. Francis of Assisi, founded the Poor Clares, a Franciscan order of nuns dedicated to strict poverty and simplicity of life.

Page 65: "Ignatius at La Storta": In his autobiography, Ignatius Loyola explains that on his way to Rome with his companions, to give themselves in obedience to the Pope, he stopped off at the small chapel of La Storta and during his prayer received, as he says, "a change in his soul and saw so clearly that God the Father had placed him with His Son...." It is from that mystical experience that Ignatius decided to call his new order of priests, "The Society of Jesus." He limped because of an injury to his leg he received as a young man in a war with France at Pamplona.

Page 67: "For Margaret Clitherow. . . ." Margaret Clitherow was born in 1556. She married John Clitherow, a butcher, in 1571 and bore him three children. Converted to Roman Catholicism in 1574, she risked her life by harboring priests during the persecution of Elizabeth I. She was arrested and refused to plead. Pregnant with her fourth child, she was executed on Good Friday, 1586, by being pressed to death. It is said Elizabeth objected to her execution because she was a woman. Margaret is often referred to as the "pearl of York." "Butcher's bloom" is a shrub that grows in Yorkshire.

Page 69: "Remembering El Salvador Jesuits. . . ." On November 16, 1989, in the early evening, government-backed military personnel rounded up six Jesuits of the Universidad Centro-Americana in San Salvador, their housekeeper and her daughter, took them into the garden of the Jesuit Residence, and there executed them by gunfire. One witness escaped to tell the story. Justice has not yet been obtained.

The Jesuits: Ignacio Ellacuria, S.J., Ignacio Martín Baró, S.J., Segundo Montes, S.J., Juan Ramón Moreno, S.J., Joaquín López y López, S.J., Amando López, S.J.

Housekeeper and daughter: Elba Ramos and Celina Ramos

Page 71: "Like Julian": Julian of Norwich (1342-1416). Her name is uncertain, but she was an anchoress, living a hermit's life in a cell attached to the Church of St. Julian in Norwich. She is famous for her lengthy work, *The Revelations of Divine Love*.

Page 72: "*Missa Solemnis*" (Solemn Mass): "Introibo ad altare Dei" ("I will go unto the altar of God"). St. Ambrose (340-397) was made Bishop of Milan, Italy, by popular acclamation. He greatly influenced St. Augustine. Sangchuan is an island off the southern coast of China, where Francis Xavier, S.J. (1506-1552), missionary, celebrated his last Mass and where he died, unable to reach the mainland.

Acknowledgments

I AM GRATEFUL FOR THE generous spirit of Arthur Liebscher, S.J., the editorial wisdom of James Torrens, S.J., the technological expertise of Paul Soukup, S.J., and the detailed reading of Charles Phipps, S.J.

Made in the USA
Columbia, SC
28 November 2017